CELEBRATING THE GRADUATION OF:

As you start your journey, the first thing you should do is throw away that store-bought map and begin to draw your own map.
– Michael Dell

Thoughts / Comments	Thoughts / Messages
NAME:_____	NAME:_____

NAME:_____	NAME:_____

 Congratulations Grad

I've learned that people will forget what you said, people will forget what you did, but people will never forget how you made them feel.
- Maya Angelou

Thoughts / Comments

NAME:_____

Thoughts / Comments

NAME:_____

NAME:_____

NAME:_____

Congratulations Grad

Be who you are and say what you feel, because those who mind don't matter and those who matter don't mind.
- Dr. Seuss

Thoughts / Messages

NAME:_____

Thoughts / Messages

NAME:_____

NAME:_____

NAME:_____

Congratulations Grad

Never settle for the path of least resistance.
- Lee Ann Womack

Thoughts / Messages

NAME:_____

Thoughts / Messages

NAME:_____

NAME:_____

NAME:_____

 Congratulations Grad

Your education is a dress rehearsal for a life that is yours to lead.
- Nora Ephron

Thoughts / Messages	Thoughts / Messages
NAME:_____	NAME:_____

NAME:_____	NAME:_____

 **Congratulations Grad**

Live in that sweet spot. Be present.
- Wynton Marsalis

Thoughts / Messages

NAME:_____

Thoughts / Messages

NAME:_____

NAME:_____

NAME:_____

Congratulations Grad

Some life lessons don't ever change. But how you embrace them will distinguish   you from the pack. *-Brooke Shields*

Thoughts / Messages	Thoughts / Messages
NAME:_____	NAME:_____

NAME:_____	NAME:_____

 **Congratulations Grad**

There will be times when your best isn't your good enough. There can be many reasons for this, but as long as you give your best you'll be OK. - *Robert DeNiro*

Thoughts / Messages

NAME:_____

Thoughts / Messages

NAME:_____

NAME:_____

NAME:_____

 Congratulations Grad

The opposite of love isn't hate. It isn't even indifference. It's fear.

- Mary Karr

Thoughts / Messages

Thoughts / Messages

NAME:_____

NAME:_____

NAME:_____

NAME:_____

Congratulations Grad

Success leads to the greatest failure, which is arrogance and pride. Failure can lead to the greatest success, which is humility and learning. *- David Brooks*

Thoughts / Messages

NAME:_____

Thoughts / Messages

NAME:_____

NAME:_____

NAME:_____

Congratulations Grad

We have the choice, the ability to acknowledge that being 'scared' is not who we are.
- Paul Glaser

Thoughts / Messages	Thoughts / Messages

NAME:_____

NAME:_____

NAME:_____

NAME:_____

Congratulations Grad

Don't ever aim your doubt at yourself. Laugh at yourself, but don't doubt yourself.
- Alan Alda

Thoughts / Messages

NAME:_____

Thoughts / Messages

NAME:_____

NAME:_____

NAME:_____

Congratulations Grad

Life is an improvisation. You have no idea what's going to happen next and you are mostly just making things up as you go along. - *Stephen Colbert*

Thoughts / Messages	Thoughts / Messages

NAME:_____

NAME:_____

NAME:_____

NAME:_____

 Congratulations Grad

Creativity is a renewable resource. Be as creative as you like, as often as you like, because you can never run out! - *Biz Stone*

Thoughts / Messages

NAME:_____

Thoughts / Messages

NAME:_____

NAME:_____

NAME:_____

 **Congratulations Grad**

You cannot authentically live anyone's life but your own. That is the deal life offers us.
- Gabrielle Giffords

Thoughts / Messages

NAME:_____

Thoughts / Messages

NAME:_____

NAME:_____

NAME:_____

 Congratulations Grad

You have nothing to lose. Everything you have acquired of value is locked inside you.
- Jerry Zucker

Thoughts / Messages

NAME:_____

Thoughts / Messages

NAME:_____

NAME:_____

NAME:_____

Congratulations Grad

Creativity is a consequence of action, not its motivation. Do what needs to be done and then ask whether it was possible. - *Wade David*

Thoughts / Messages	Thoughts / Messages

NAME:_____

NAME:_____

NAME:_____

NAME:_____

 **Congratulations Grad**

For the most important decisions in your life, trust your intuition, and then work with everything you have, to prove it right. - *TIM COOK*

Thoughts / Messages

NAME:_____

Thoughts / Messages

NAME:_____

NAME:_____

NAME:_____

 **Congratulations Grad**

You will have failures in your life, but it is what you do during those valleys that will determine the heights of your peaks. - *RAHM EMANUEL*

Thoughts / Messages	Thoughts / Messages
NAME:_____	NAME:_____

NAME:_____	NAME:_____

 **Congratulations Grad**

Just remember, you can't climb the ladder of success with your hands in your pockets.
- ARNOLD SCHWARZENEGGER

Thoughts / Messages

NAME:_____

Thoughts / Messages

NAME:_____

NAME:_____

NAME:_____

 **Congratulations Grad**

When people tell you not to believe in your dreams, and they say "Why?", say "Why not?"
- BILLIE JEAN KING

Thoughts / Messages

NAME:_____

Thoughts / Messages

NAME:_____

NAME:_____

NAME:_____

Congratulations Grad

I know that luck has a way of happening to people who shoot high, who never sell themselves short. - *TERI TEACHOUT*

Thoughts / Messages

NAME:_____

Thoughts / Messages

NAME:_____

NAME:_____

NAME:_____

 **Congratulations Grad**

The great and curious truth of the human experience is that selflessness is the best thing you can do for yourself. - *DAVID MCCULLOUGH JR*

Thoughts / Messages

NAME:_____

Thoughts / Messages

NAME:_____

NAME:_____

NAME:_____

Congratulations Grad

As you start your journey, the first thing you should do is throw away that store-bought map and begin to draw your own. -- *MICHAEL DELL*

Thoughts / Messages

NAME:_____

Thoughts / Messages

NAME:_____

NAME:_____

NAME:_____

 Congratulations Grad

Sucess is like a mountain that keeps growing ahead of you as you hike it.. Err in the direction of kindness.

-- GEORGE SAUNDERS

Thoughts / Messages

NAME:_____

Thoughts / Messages

NAME:_____

NAME:_____

NAME:_____

Congratulations Grad

There is nothing a person can't do, and there should be nothing a human being didn't care about It was the most positive encouragement I could have hoped for.- *Maya Angelou*

Thoughts / Messages

NAME:_____

Thoughts / Messages

NAME:_____

NAME:_____

NAME:_____

Congratulations Grad

The future lies before you like a field of driven snow, be careful how you tread it, for every step will show. *-Author Unknown*

Thoughts / Messages

NAME:_____

Thoughts / Messages

NAME:_____

NAME:_____

NAME:_____

Congratulations Grad

If you want your life to count, you have to focus on it. You don't have time for everything, and not everything is of equal value. *- Rick Warren*

Thoughts / Messages

NAME:_____

Thoughts / Messages

NAME:_____

NAME:_____

NAME:_____

 Congratulations Grad

The future lies before you like a field of driven snow, be careful how you tread it, for every step will show. *-Author Unknown*

Thoughts / Messages

NAME:_____

Thoughts / Messages

NAME:_____

NAME:_____

NAME:_____

 **Congratulations Grad**

If you want your life to count, you have to focus it. You don't have time for everything, and not everything is of equal value.- *Rick Warren*

Thoughts / Messages	Thoughts / Messages
NAME:_____	NAME:_____

NAME:_____	NAME:_____

 **Congratulations Grad**

Shoot for the moon! Even if you miss...you'll land among the stars.
- Les Brown

Thoughts / Messages	Thoughts / Messages

NAME:_____

NAME:_____

NAME:_____

NAME:_____

 Congratulations Grad

Be who you are and say what you feel, because those who mind don't matter and those who matter don't mind.- *Dr. Seuss*

Thoughts / Messages

NAME:_____

Thoughts / Messages

NAME:_____

NAME:_____

NAME:_____

Congratulations Grad

At commencement you wear your square-shaped mortarboards. My hope is that from time to time you will let your minds be bold, and wear sombreros.- *Paul Freund*

Thoughts / Messages

Thoughts / Messages

NAME:_____

NAME:_____

NAME:_____

NAME:_____

Congratulations Grad

Sending you a day full of sunshine, a heaven filled with rainbows, and a pocket full of dreams. May the future ahead of you be as wonderful as you are.- Judith *Wibberley*

Thoughts / Messages

NAME:_____

Thoughts / Messages

NAME:_____

NAME:_____

NAME:_____

 Congratulations Grad

> Graduation is only a concept. In real life every day you graduate. Graduation is a process that goes on until the last day of your life. If you can grasp that, you'll make a difference.
> *- Arie Pencovici*

Thoughts / Messages

NAME:_____

Thoughts / Messages

NAME:_____

NAME:_____

NAME:_____

Congratulations Grad

You may never know what results come of your action, but if you do nothing there will be no result.- *Mahatma Ghandi*

Thoughts / Messages	Thoughts / Messages
NAME:_____	NAME:_____

NAME:_____	NAME:_____

 **Congratulations Grad**

Success is going from failure to failure without losing your enthusiasm.
- Sir Winston Churchill

Thoughts / Messages

NAME:_____

Thoughts / Messages

NAME:_____

NAME:_____

NAME:_____

Congratulations Grad

Wherever you go, no matter what the weather, always bring your own sunshine.
-Anthony J. D'Angelo

Thoughts / Messages

NAME:_____

Thoughts / Messages

NAME:_____

NAME:_____

NAME:_____

 Congratulations Grad

You can become someone who is worthy of respect, and someone who can pursue what he wants irrespective of what others say or do. *-Faith Starr*

Thoughts / Messages

NAME:_____

Thoughts / Messages

NAME:_____

NAME:_____

NAME:_____

 **Congratulations Grad**

Knowledge is meaningful only if it is reflected in action. The human race has found out the hard way that we are what we do, not just what we think. *-Robert Fulghum*

Thoughts / Messages

NAME:_____

Thoughts / Messages

NAME:_____

NAME:_____

NAME:_____

Congratulations Grad

Your parents, proudly here today, and their parents before them, perhaps proudly here today, understood a simple equation for success: your children would do better than you had.
- Anna Quindlen

Thoughts / Comments

NAME:_____

Thoughts / Comments

NAME:_____

NAME:_____

NAME:_____

 **Congratulations Grad**

You can complain about the direction of your life all you want, but until you sit in the driver's seat and begin to drive yourself, you aren't going to get where you want to go!- Les Brown

Thoughts / Messages	Thoughts / Messages

NAME:_____

NAME:_____

NAME:_____

NAME:_____

 **Congratulations Grad**

Graduation day is finally here, your dreams you did pursue. All your hard work has paid off, we are so very proud of you. *- Catherine Pulsifer*

Thoughts / Messages

NAME:_____

Thoughts / Messages

NAME:_____

NAME:_____

NAME:_____

 **Congratulations Grad**

The larger the island of knowledge, the longer the shoreline of wonder.
- Ralph W. Sockman

Thoughts / Messages

NAME:_____

Thoughts / Messages

NAME:_____

NAME:_____

NAME:_____

 **Congratulations Grad**

The future belongs to those who believe in the beauty of their dreams.
- Eleanor Roosevelt

Thoughts / Messages

NAME:_____

Thoughts / Messages

NAME:_____

NAME:_____

NAME:_____

 Congratulations Grad

The most rewarding things in life are often the ones that look like they cannot be done.
- Arnold Palmer

Thoughts / Messages

NAME:_____

Thoughts / Messages

NAME:_____

NAME:_____

NAME:_____

Congratulations Grad

If you aren't fired with enthusiasm, you will be fired with enthusiasm.
- Vince Lombardi

Thoughts / Messages

NAME:_____

Thoughts / Messages

NAME:_____

NAME:_____

NAME:_____

Congratulations Grad

Things turn out best for the people who make the best out of the way things turn out.
- Art Linkletter

Thoughts / Messages

NAME:_____

Thoughts / Messages

NAME:_____

NAME:_____

NAME:_____

 **Congratulations Grad**

The best of all things is to learn. Money can be lost or stolen, health and strength may fail, but what you have committed to your mind is yours forever.- *Louis L'Amour*

Thoughts / Messages	Thoughts / Messages
NAME:_____	NAME:_____

NAME:_____	NAME:_____

 **Congratulations Grad**

The fireworks begin today. Each diploma is a lighted match. Each one of you is a fuse.
- Edward Koch

Thoughts / Comments

NAME:_____

Thoughts / Comments

NAME:_____

NAME:_____

NAME:_____

Congratulations Grad

I believe in the principle that I can make a difference in this world. It may be ever so small, but it will count for the greater good.- *Gordon B. Hinckley*

Thoughts / Messages

NAME:_____

Thoughts / Messages

NAME:_____

NAME:_____

NAME:_____

 Congratulations Grad

It is not the mountain we conquer but ourselves.
-Edmund Hillary

Thoughts / Messages

NAME:_____

Thoughts / Messages

NAME:_____

NAME:_____

NAME:_____

Congratulations Grad

Patience, persistence and perspiration make an unbeatable combination for success.
- Napoleon Hill

Thoughts / Messages

NAME:_____

Thoughts / Messages

NAME:_____

NAME:_____

NAME:_____

Congratulations Grad

The true meaning of life is to plant trees, under whose shade you do not expect to sit.
- Nelson Henderson

Thoughts / Messages

NAME:_____

Thoughts / Messages

NAME:_____

NAME:_____

NAME:_____

 Congratulations Grad

The whole purpose of education is to turn mirrors into windows.
- Sydney J. Harris

Thoughts / Messages

NAME:_____

Thoughts / Messages

NAME:_____

NAME:_____

NAME:_____

Congratulations Grad

Success isn't a result of spontaneous combustion. You must set yourself on fire.
- Arnold H. Glasow

Thoughts / Messages

NAME:_____

Thoughts / Messages

NAME:_____

NAME:_____

NAME:_____

 **Congratulations Grad**

Obstacles are those frightful things you see when you take your eyes off your goal.
- Henry Ford

Thoughts / Messages

NAME:_____

Thoughts / Messages

NAME:_____

NAME:_____

NAME:_____

Congratulations Grad

There is just one life for each of us: our own.
- Euripides

Thoughts / Messages

NAME:_____

Thoughts / Messages

NAME:_____

NAME:_____

NAME:_____

Congratulations Grad

The things taught in schools and colleges are not an education, but the means of education. *-Ralph Waldo Emerson*

Thoughts / Messages	Thoughts / Messages
NAME:_____	NAME:_____

NAME:_____	NAME:_____

 **Congratulations Grad**

The important thing is not to stop questioning.
- Albert Einstein

Thoughts / Messages

NAME:_____

Thoughts / Messages

NAME:_____

NAME:_____

NAME:_____

 Congratulations Grad

The important thing is this: to be able to give up in any given moment all that we are for what we can become.- *DeSeaux*

Thoughts / Messages	Thoughts / Messages
NAME:_____	NAME:_____

NAME:_____	NAME:_____

 **Congratulations Grad**

The best helping hand that you will ever receive is the one at the end of your own arm.
- Fred Dehner

Thoughts / Messages

NAME:_____

Thoughts / Messages

NAME:_____

NAME:_____

NAME:_____

 Congratulations Grad

It takes courage to grow up and become who you really are.
- E.E. Cummings

Thoughts / Messages

NAME:_____

Thoughts / Messages

NAME:_____

NAME:_____

NAME:_____

 **Congratulations Grad**

Success is the ability to go from one failure to another with no loss of enthusiasm.
- Winston Churchill

Thoughts / Messages

NAME:_____

Thoughts / Messages

NAME:_____

NAME:_____

NAME:_____

 Congratulations Grad

Shoot for the moon. Even if you miss, you'll land among the stars.
- Les Brown

Thoughts / Messages

NAME:_____

Thoughts / Messages

NAME:_____

NAME:_____

NAME:_____

 **Congratulations Grad**

Think big thoughts but relish small pleasures.
-H. Jackson Brown, Jr.

Thoughts / Messages

NAME:_____

Thoughts / Messages

NAME:_____

NAME:_____

NAME:_____

Congratulations Grad

If opportunity doesn't knock, build a door.
- Milton Berle

Thoughts / Messages

NAME:_____

Thoughts / Messages

NAME:_____

NAME:_____

NAME:_____

 **Congratulations Grad**

Keep in mind that neither success nor failure is ever final.
-Roger Babson

Thoughts / Messages

NAME:_____

Thoughts / Messages

NAME:_____

NAME:_____

NAME:_____

 **Congratulations Grad**

Who you are tomorrow begins with who you are today.
– Tim Fargo

Thoughts / Comments	Thoughts / Messages

NAME:_____

NAME:_____

NAME:_____

NAME:_____

 **Congratulations Grad**

Put your heart, mind, and soul into even your smallest acts. This is the secret of success.
- Swami Sivananda

Thoughts / Comments

NAME:_____

Thoughts / Comments

NAME:_____

NAME:_____

NAME:_____

 Congratulations Grad

Success is not in what you have, but who you are
- Bo Bennett

Thoughts / Messages

NAME:_____

Thoughts / Messages

NAME:_____

NAME:_____

NAME:_____

 Congratulations Grad

Accomplishment will prove to be a journey, not a destination.

- Dwight D. Eisenhower

Thoughts / Messages

NAME:_____

Thoughts / Messages

NAME:_____

NAME:_____

NAME:_____

Congratulations Grad

Your education is a dress rehearsal for a life that is yours to lead.
- Nora Ephron

Thoughts / Messages

NAME:_____

Thoughts / Messages

NAME:_____

NAME:_____

NAME:_____

Congratulations Grad

Believe you can and you are half way there.
- Theodore Roosevelt

Thoughts / Messages

NAME:_____

Thoughts / Messages

NAME:_____

NAME:_____

NAME:_____

 **Congratulations Grad**

Keep your face always towards the sunshine and shadows will fall behind you
-Walt Whitman

Thoughts / Messages

NAME:_____

Thoughts / Messages

NAME:_____

NAME:_____

NAME:_____

Congratulations Grad

To succeed in life you need two things: Ignorance and confidence.
- Mark Twain

Thoughts / Messages

NAME:_____

Thoughts / Messages

NAME:_____

NAME:_____

NAME:_____

Congratulations Grad

Work hard in silence, let your success be your noise.
- Frank Ocean

Thoughts / Messages

NAME:_____

Thoughts / Messages

NAME:_____

NAME:_____

NAME:_____

 **Congratulations Grad**

Success leads to the greatest failure, which is arrogance and pride. Failure can lead to the greatest success, which is humility and learning. *- David Brooks*

Thoughts / Messages

NAME:_____

Thoughts / Messages

NAME:_____

NAME:_____

NAME:_____

Congratulations Grad

We have the choice, the ability to acknowledge that being 'scared' is not who we are.
- Paul Glaser

Thoughts / Messages

NAME:_____

Thoughts / Messages

NAME:_____

NAME:_____

NAME:_____

Congratulations Grad

Don't ever aim your doubt at yourself. Laugh at yourself, but don't doubt yourself.
- Alan Alda

Thoughts / Messages

NAME:_____

Thoughts / Messages

NAME:_____

NAME:_____

NAME:_____

 *Congratulations Grad*

Life is an improvisation. You have no idea what's going to happen next and you are mostly just making things up as you go along. *- Stephen Colbert*

Thoughts / Messages

NAME:_____

Thoughts / Messages

NAME:_____

NAME:_____

NAME:_____

 Congratulations Grad

Creativity is a renewable resource. Be as creative as you like, as often as you like, because you can never run out! - *Biz Stone*

Thoughts / Messages

NAME:_____

Thoughts / Messages

NAME:_____

NAME:_____

NAME:_____

Congratulations Grad

Congratulations Grad

Congratulations Grad

Congratulations Grad

Congratulations Grad

Congratulations Grad

Congratulations Grad

GIFT LOG

DATE	GIFT DESCRIPTION	GIVEN BY	THANK YOU NOTICE SENT

GIFT LOG

DATE	GIFT DESCRIPTION	GIVEN BY	THANK YOU NOTICE SENT

GIFT LOG

DATE	GIFT DESCRIPTION	GIVEN BY	THANK YOU NOTICE SENT

GIFT LOG

DATE	GIFT DESCRIPTION	GIVEN BY	THANK YOU NOTICE SENT

GIFT LOG

DATE	GIFT DESCRIPTION	GIVEN BY	THANK YOU NOTICE SENT

GIFT LOG

DATE	GIFT DESCRIPTION	GIVEN BY	THANK YOU NOTICE SENT

GIFT LOG

DATE	GIFT DESCRIPTION	GIVEN BY	THANK YOU NOTICE SENT

GIFT LOG

DATE	GIFT DESCRIPTION	GIVEN BY	THANK YOU NOTICE SENT

GIFT LOG

DATE	GIFT DESCRIPTION	GIVEN BY	THANK YOU NOTICE SENT

GIFT LOG

DATE	GIFT DESCRIPTION	GIVEN BY	THANK YOU NOTICE SENT

GIFT LOG

DATE	GIFT DESCRIPTION	GIVEN BY	THANK YOU NOTICE SENT

GIFT LOG

DATE	GIFT DESCRIPTION	GIVEN BY	THANK YOU NOTICE SENT

GIFT LOG

DATE	GIFT DESCRIPTION	GIVEN BY	THANK YOU NOTICE SENT

GIFT LOG

DATE	GIFT DESCRIPTION	GIVEN BY	THANK YOU NOTICE SENT

GIFT LOG

DATE	GIFT DESCRIPTION	GIVEN BY	THANK YOU NOTICE SENT

GIFT LOG

DATE	GIFT DESCRIPTION	GIVEN BY	THANK YOU NOTICE SENT

Made in the USA
Coppell, TX
27 March 2024

30614948R00067